SPARK

Drawing exercises that ignite team creativity

Matteo, Milena, Michela
and Valerio Zanini

5D Vision Publishing

Spark
Drawing exercises that ignite team creativity

Matteo Zanini, Milena Zanini, Michela Zanini, Valerio Zanini
Copyright © 2017, 2018, 2021

We plant one tree for every copy of this book sold, in partnership with ForestPlanet.org

Third edition
Printed in the United States of America

Cover image: freepik.com Premium license

ISBN : 978-0-9989854-0-4

Published by:
5D Vision Publishing, an imprint of 5D Vision, LLC
Washington, DC - USA

Web: www.5dvision.com
Email: info@5dvision.com

SPARK

**Drawing exercises that
ignite team creativity**

Introduction

I have found that creative drawing is a terrific way to really jump start peoples' brains and usually share some laughs, which both promotes creativity and lowers peoples' defenses and fear of judgment. This is particularly important in sessions that require actual brainstorming, and applies as well to any team building setting, including project kickoffs and retrospectives.

The idea behind this book

Over the years, I have facilitated many brainstorming and team building sessions with a variety of teams. Sometimes these sessions occurred with a diverse group of people, who had never worked together, and often had not even met each other before. The challenge was always to create a sense of team, to get people comfortable working together, and to minimize any impediment to sharing ideas freely.

Often, these meetings start with some sort of icebreaker to quickly establish a social connection and lower psychological barriers to working with each other. The Internet and the bookstores are full of examples of effective icebreakers, and I have tried many different kinds.

Many of these icebreakers involve everyone going around the room and sharing their favorite band, the book they are currently reading, or the like. These exercises can be effective in bringing people closer together, but they also have limitations. Personally, during those types of exercises my attention inevitably wanders to planning what I am going to say when it's my turn. Then, after I have shared my story and others are talking, I keep thinking about what I just said, and how I could have delivered it better. When the exercise is over, I may have really listened to only a handful of stories, and five minutes later most memories of what anyone said are gone.

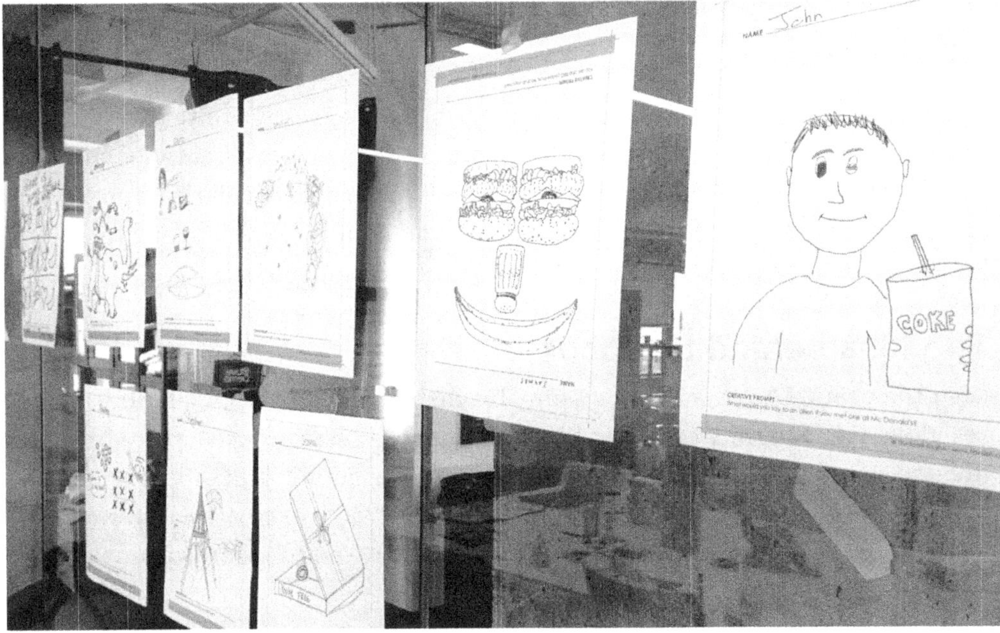

So, I like to do something a bit different to really get peoples' creative juices flowing and render the experience more interesting and memorable.

This book brings together many ideas from all the icebreaker/creative drawing experiments I have conducted over the years, in a simple format. I ask that everyone draws something related to a story about them or some aspect of their lives, so that through the drawing the artist is sharing a personal element with the team. Sometimes, there is a true Picasso in the group, but most people are not talented artists. The value of the exercise lies in the process, not the quality of the product.

The act of drawing engages the right side of the brain, and it mixes visual, verbal, and kinesthetic experiences, so it works for various types of learning styles. The drawing process can be unnerving, and will undoubtedly push many beyond their comfort zone. This process in itself creates a bond amongst the participants, as they all confront a common challenge. Once the drawing is complete, a great deal of the psychological pressure has passed. Presenting the drawing is then relatively easy because the drawing is already complete and cannot be changed. It is therefore easier to listen fully to others. The final step is to post all the drawings on the wall so that they remain visible throughout the session and people can remember what another team member drew and why.

How to use this book

These are drawing exercises for teams of any size. The ideal exercise takes between 10 and 15 minutes depending on the team's size. I recommend conducting it right before a creative session like brainstorming or prototype design. Include everyone on the team – you too. Everyone gets to draw, and to share with everyone else.

Each page has a different exercise. Randomly pick a page, or select your favorite. Your task is to complete the drawing on the page, using any of the elements already present on page.

Ideally, you can draw something from a personal experience that you feel comfortable sharing with others. If you cannot come up with an idea for your drawing, next to each page is a **creative prompt**: this provides some directions to get you started. Think of the creative prompt as brain vitamins to spark your creativity. You don't have to follow the creative prompt if you don't want to, it's just there to help you if you need it. When done, write your name or you artwork's name at the top and wait for everyone else to finish.

For teams of 2-12 people

Everyone gets a page of the book. Tear it off and place it in front of you with a marker, a pen, or a crayon. When everyone is ready, start drawing.

Give everyone time to complete their drawing. Too long and the exercise loses appeal. Too short and people may not have enough time to draw anything useful. I find it best to give between 4 and 7 minutes.

Then, one by one, people stand up, walk to a nearby wall, tape their drawing to the wall, and describe it to the rest of the team. Once everyone is done describing, leave the drawings on the wall as people may refer to them later and bring up memories of the stories heard.

For large teams (more than 12 people)

The exercise can be conducted with teams of any size. Give each person a page from the book, and something to write on it. Then timebox the drawing part to just a few minutes (between 4 and 7 minutes).

Once everyone is ready to share, break the room in smaller teams, for example in groups of 5, or one team per table. Have each person share their drawing within their team. If possible, tape the drawings to the wall, next to each team.

For individuals (just you)

You can use the drawing exercises in this book on your own, to spark your creativity or to overcome boredom during long meetings. And if your boss catches you, just explain that you are working on your Sparks!

When to use the Sparks

The Spark exercises can be used in a variety of settings. Here are some ideas for different contexts:

Team liftoff

For new teams, get to know each other, break the ice, expand comfort zone

Meeting kickoff

For new or existing teams, break the ice, create safe space to share ideas

Team building

For people that work together, expand comfort zone, keep building shared memories

Class kickoff

For people that don't know each other, break the ice, make quick introductions

Retrospective

Warm up the brain juices, create a safe space to share ideas, complete a small challenge together

Product brainstorming

Spark creativity, create safe space to share ideas, use the exercises to brainstorm features or new ideas

These drawings were shared by some of our readers, and are reproduced here as examples.

These drawings were shared by some of our readers, and are reproduced here as examples.

Acknowledgements

I designed these exercises with the help of my kids Matteo, Milena, and Michela. After all, they are the creative brains in my house. We spent days drawing images and developing the creative prompts. They tested some of the drawings and gave me their thumbs up to move ahead with publication.

No big project can come to fruition without the support of those around you. I am thankful to the friends and colleagues that supported me throughout this journey, and in particular to my wife Deborah for continuously believing in me.

An finally, I am thankful to my parents Roberto and Maria for inspiring me to be creative and to build new things since I was a little kid.

I hope you like using these exercises as much as we liked putting it all together. Enjoy your Spark creativity!

Valerio Zanini

CREATIVE PROMPT

What is the ugliest present you ever received?

IDEA
NAME

CREATIVE PROMPT

What would you bring to a BBQ on an iceberg?

IDEA
NAME

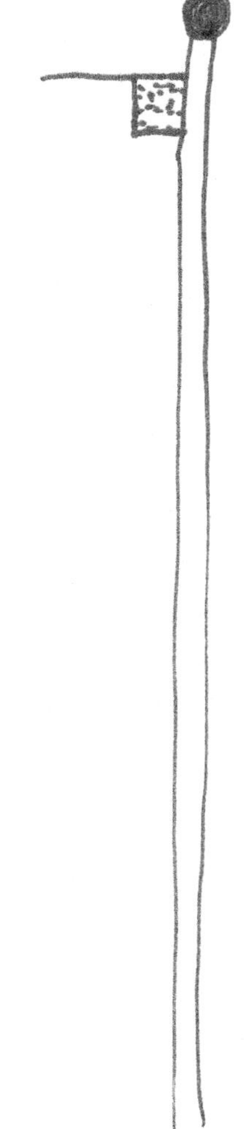

How could you help an elf stuck on top of the Eiffel tower?

NAME

CREATIVE PROMPT

During a visit to Disney Land, you get lost inside the Magic Maze. Who helps you escape?

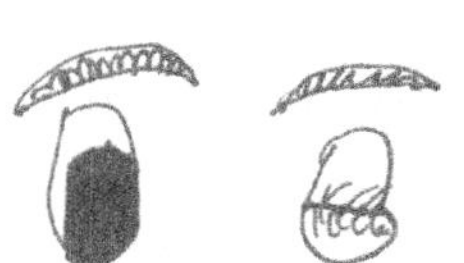

You are a gladiator preparing to go into battle. What's your secret weapon?

IDEA
NAME

CREATIVE PROMPT

What's the biggest castle you have been to?

NAME

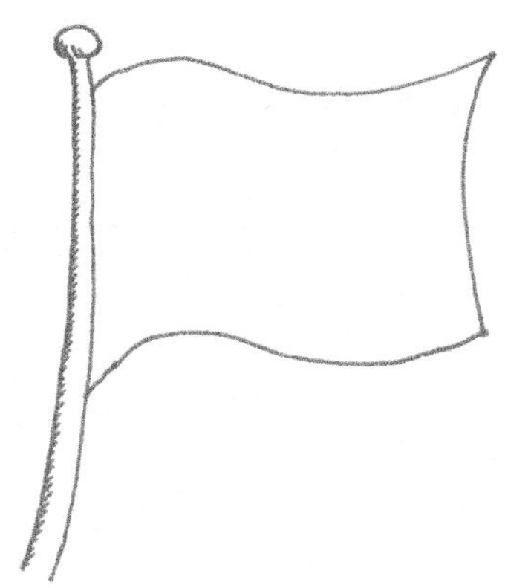

How can you run faster than the Easter Bunny?

IDEA
NAME

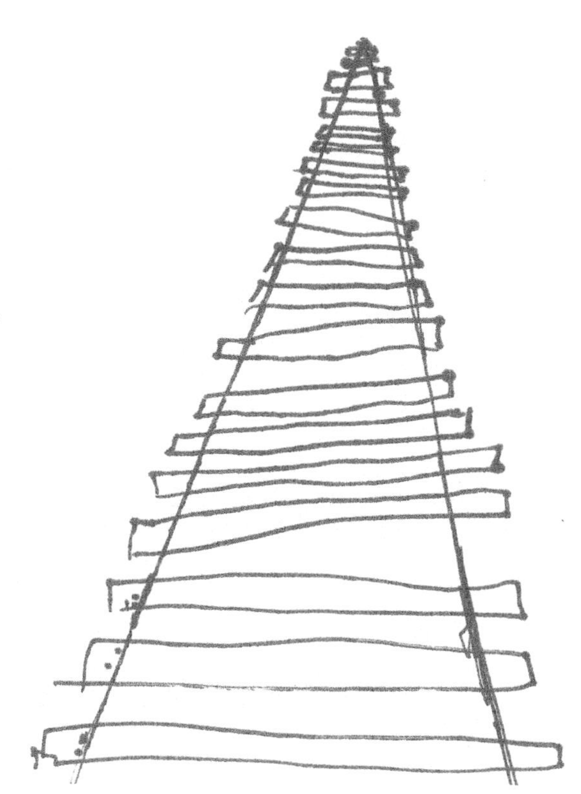

CREATIVE PROMPT

You are visiting the zoo. Take a selfie with your favorite animal.

CREATIVE PROMPT

Can you build a tree house? Can you add an elevator and a swimming pool? How can you make it really memorable?

Spark

How would you celebrate your fanciest birthday?

IDEA
NAME

CREATIVE PROMPT

How would you imagine a trip aboard the Orient Express?

NAME

Cl
ag
Cag

NAME

CREATIVE PROMPT

What is a Halloween decoration you have never seen around?

IDEA
NAME

CREATIVE PROMPT

What's the scariest thing you ever did on a mountain?

GIDEA
NAME

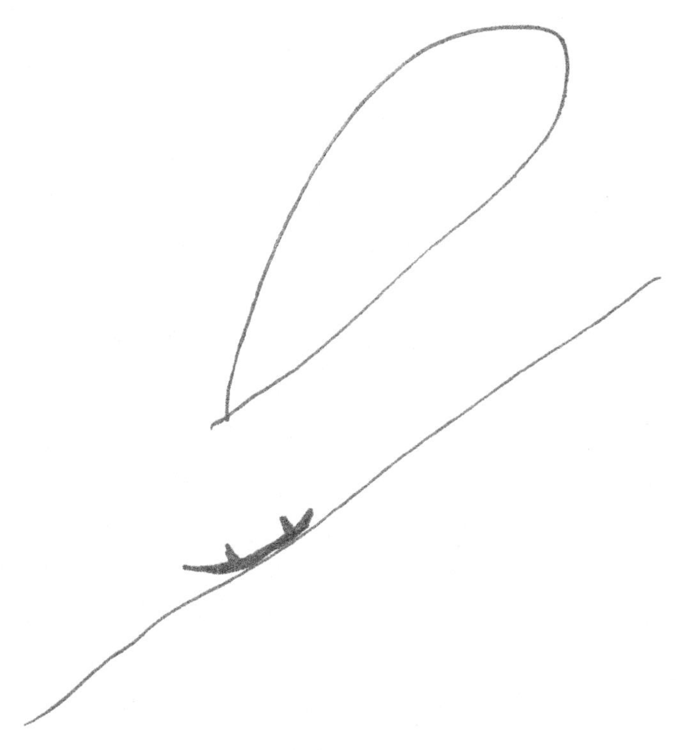

What would your car look like if there were no roads?

IDEA
NAME

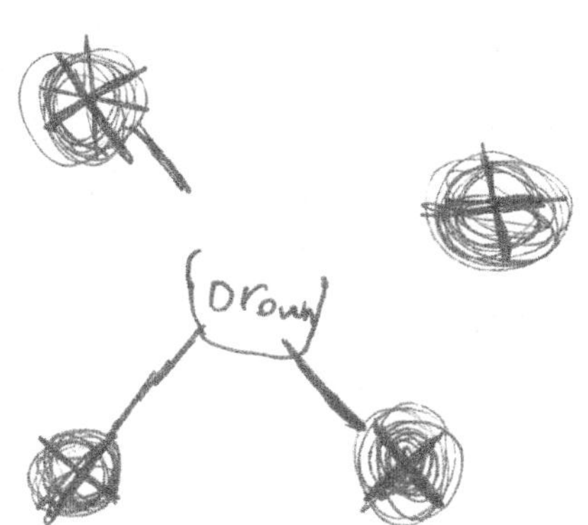

Drown

This is a present you have never received. What's inside?

NAME

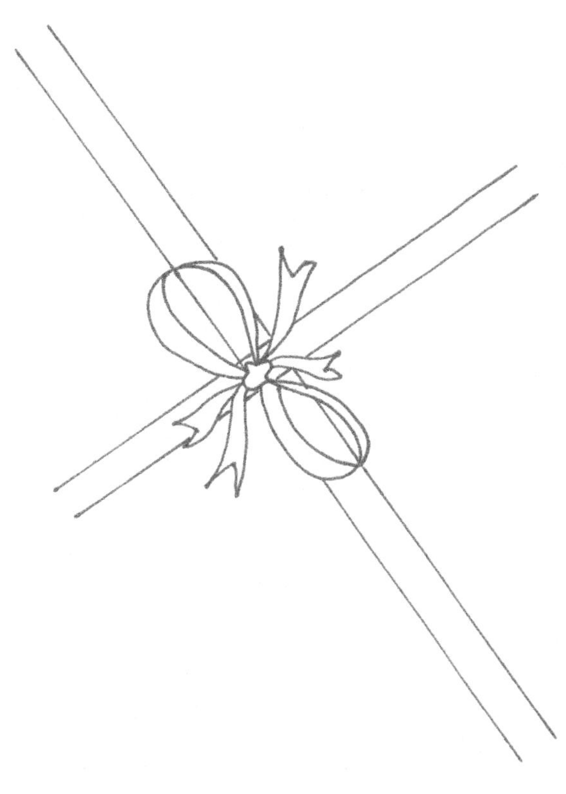

Congratulations! You just won a cruise on the Mississippi river

What animals would you include in a small zoo for your neighborhood?

IDEA
NAME

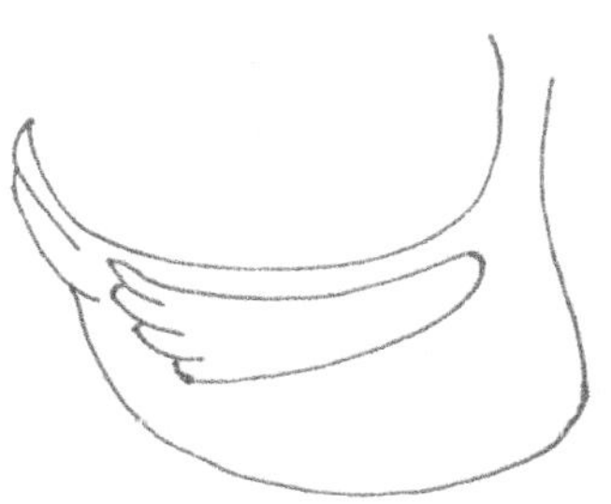

What would your home look like if it was flying on a cloud?

IDEA
NAME

CREATIVE PROMPT

How would you design your personal water park?

IDEA
NAME

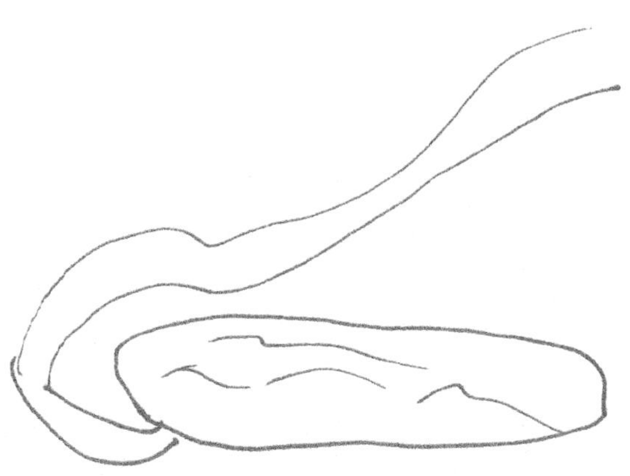

CREATIVE PROMPT

Is this an alien, a bucket full of candies, or a fancy dress?

IDEA
NAME

Create your own music band with at least 5 different instruments

IDEA
NAME

CREATIVE PROMPT

You just landed on the Moon. What does it look like?

NAME

CREATIVE PROMPT

What would your home look like if it was flying in the clouds?

IDEA
NAME

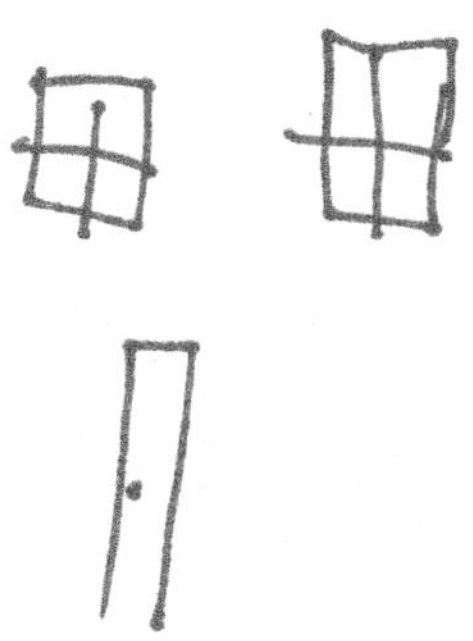

What is one thing you would take with you on a trip to Mars?

Spark

CREATIVE PROMPT

Create your ideal birthday party

IDEA
NAME

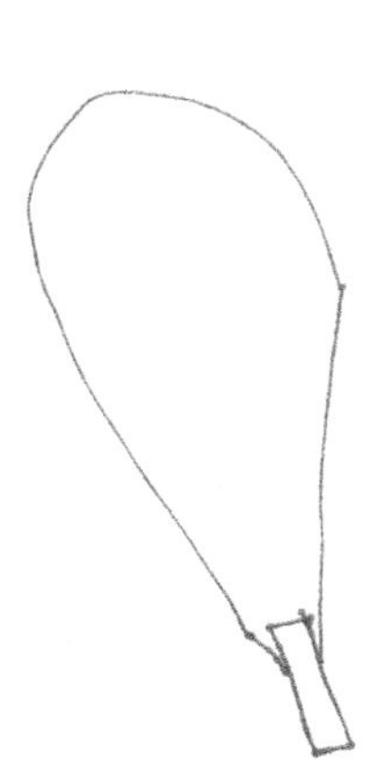

What was your favorite dinosaur growing up?

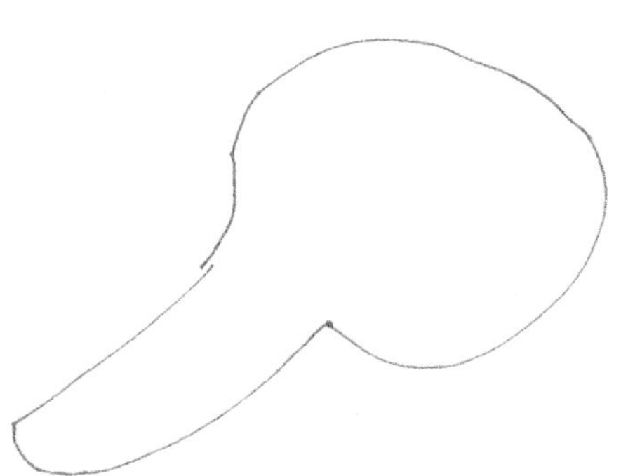

Spark

CREATIVE PROMPT

What recipe would you cook if you only had cereals, ketchup and caramel apples?

IDEA
NAME

cereal
win
$5,000
see back
for deat

CREATIVE PROMPT

What's the first thing you'd buy if you win the lottery?

X is wining -Jay

CREATIVE PROMPT

What is an activity you like to do that nobody else knows?

57

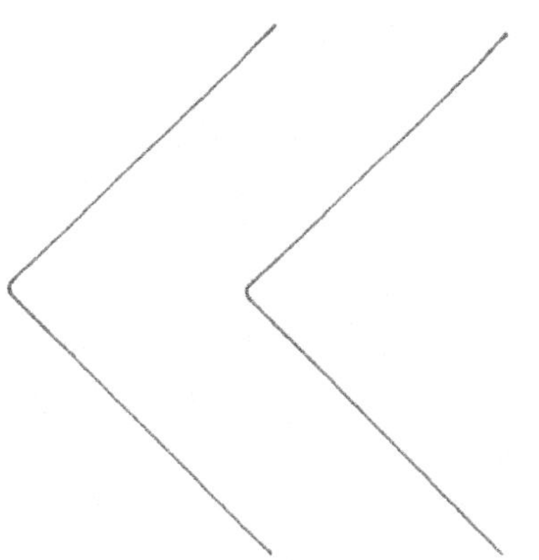

NAME

CREATIVE PROMPT

A sign along the highway is advertising your favorite drink. What does it look like?

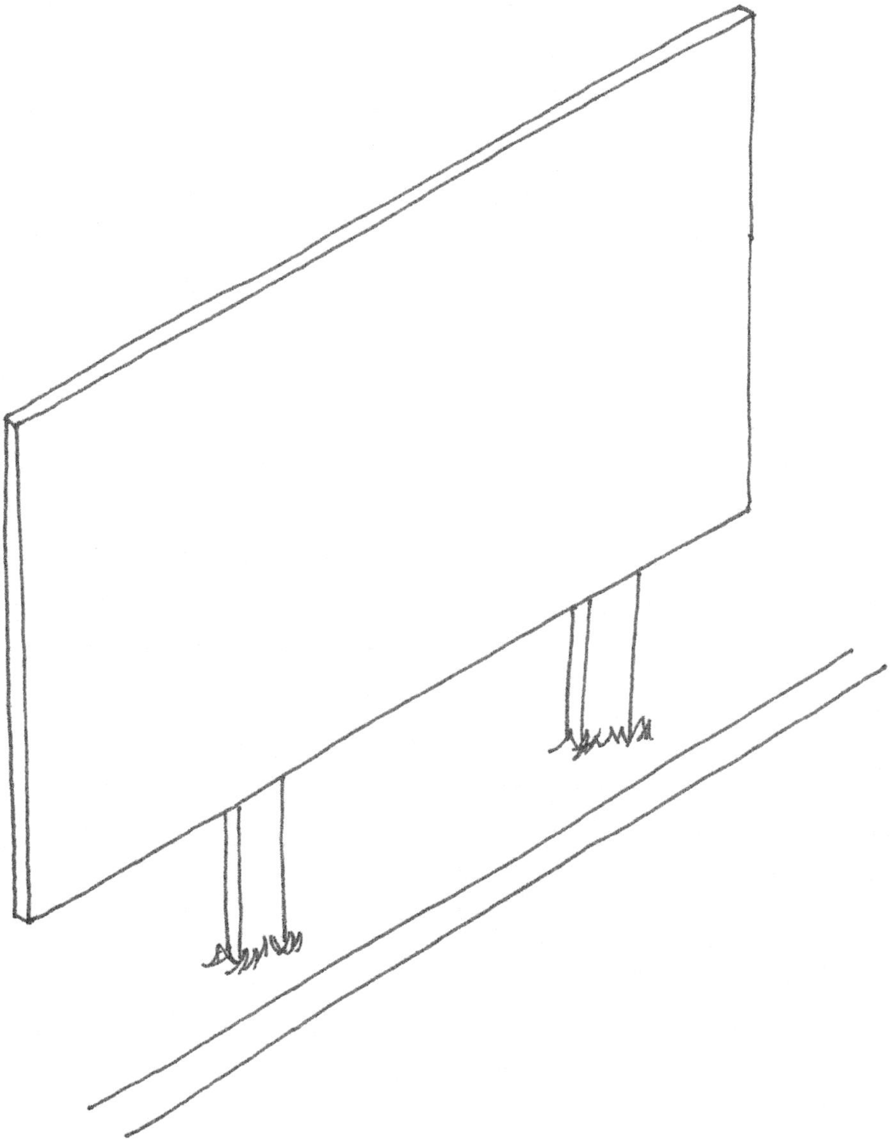

NAME

IDEA

CREATIVE PROMPT

What is your favorite beach activity?

gIDEA
NAME

CREATIVE PROMPT

What's the craziest outfit you have ever worn?

IDEA
NAME

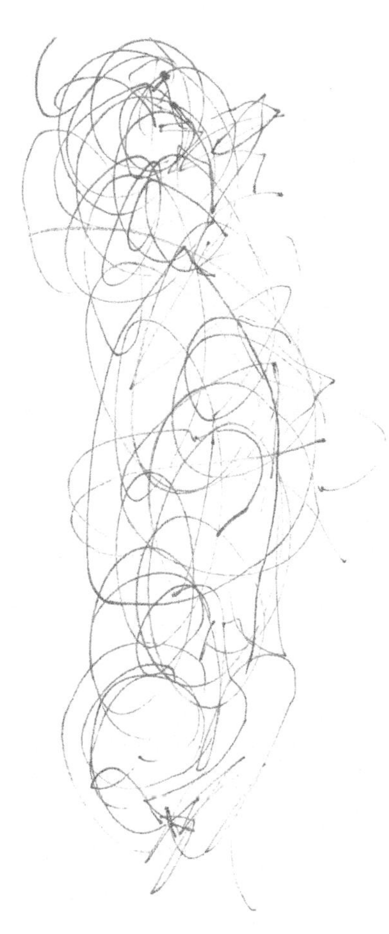

CREATIVE PROMPT

You are on a cross-country train trip. What do you see outside the windows?

NAME

Cl
ag
Cag

You found this at the grocery store. What can it be?

IDEA
NAME

CREATIVE PROMPT

What would you pack for a trip around the world?

Spark

CREATIVE PROMPT

What is the most precious thing you ever owned?

IDEA
NAME

Police

CREATIVE PROMPT

You are spending the weekend in Paris. Create postcards for three of your friends.

IDEA
NAME

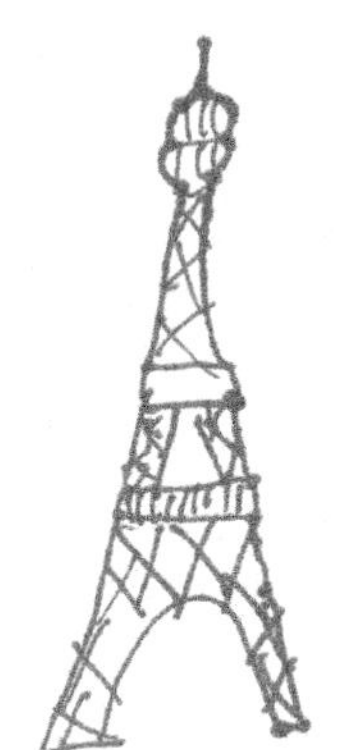

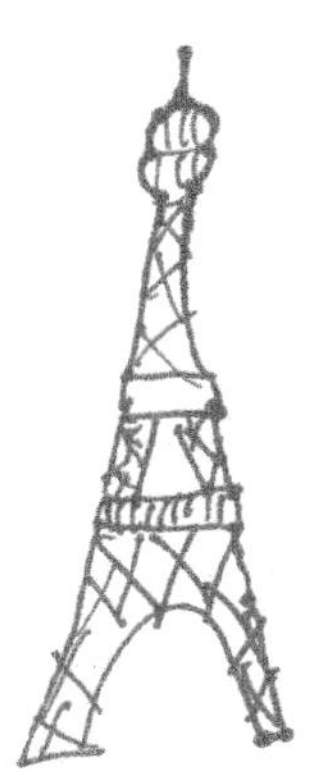

CREATIVE PROMPT

What else would Picasso have on his desk?

IDEA
NAME

CREATIVE PROMPT

Describe the tastiest food you can make with honey

IDEA
NAME

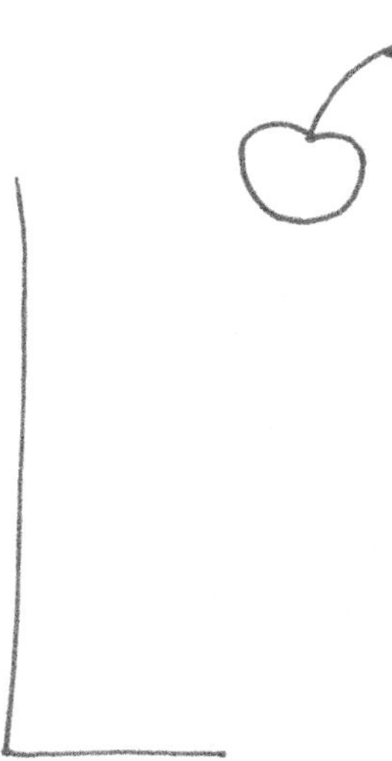

CREATIVE PROMPT

What would you find in an Amazon shipping box if your dreams come true?

NAME

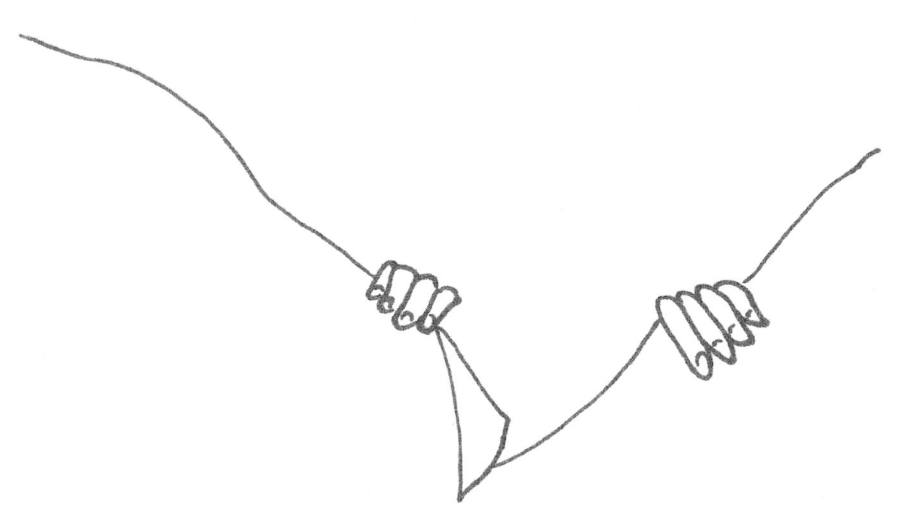

CREATIVE PROMPT

How would you make a holiday decoration with a piece of paper, a lightbulb, and a radio that only plays Rock 'n' Roll?

NAME

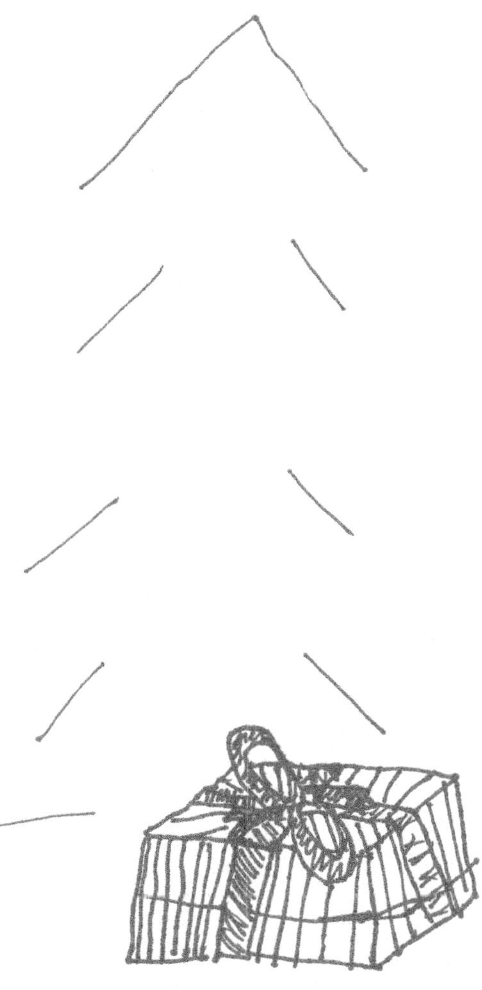

CREATIVE PROMPT

You are at a BBQ competition. What do you cook?

IDEA
NAME

CREATIVE PROMPT

How can you run faster than the Easter Bunny?

NAME

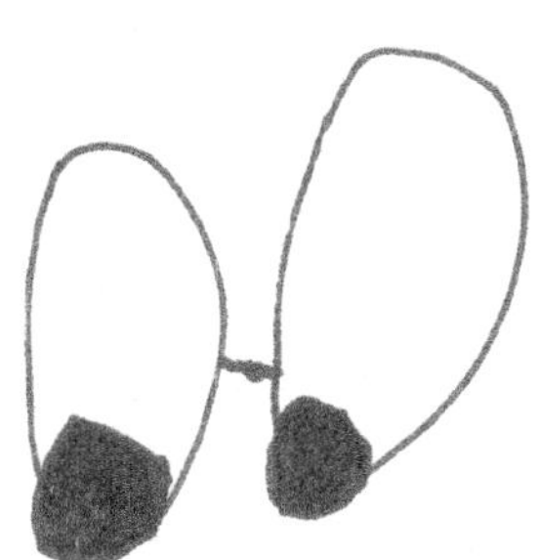

CREATIVE PROMPT

How would you cross a canyon without a bridge?

IDEA
NAME

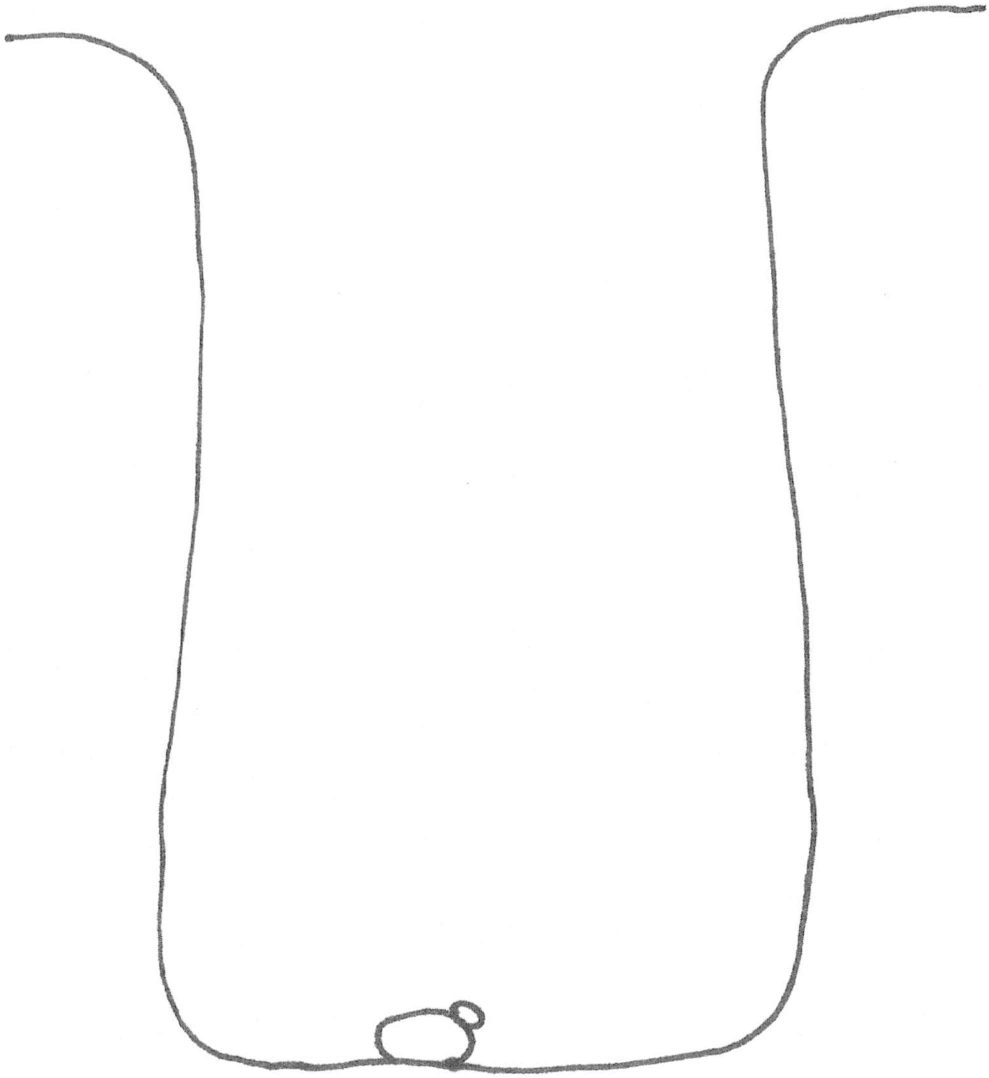

CREATIVE PROMPT

What would your home look like if there was no gravity?

NAME

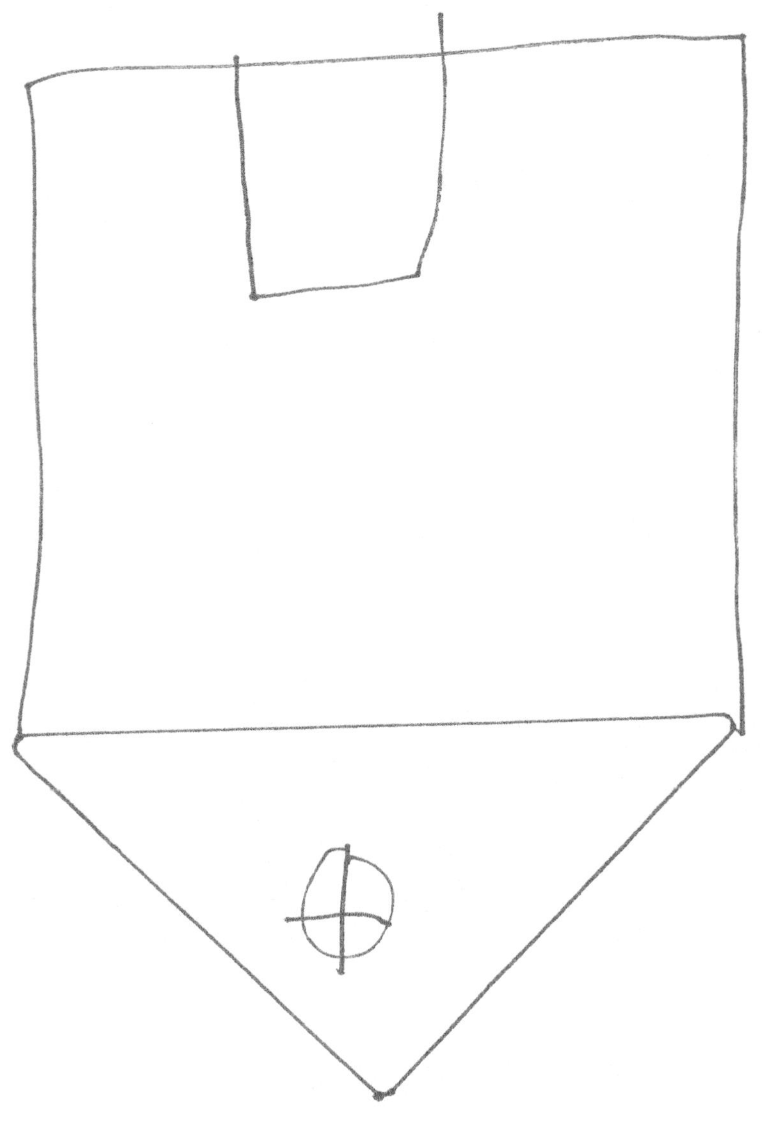

What would the craziest stuntman do?

NAME

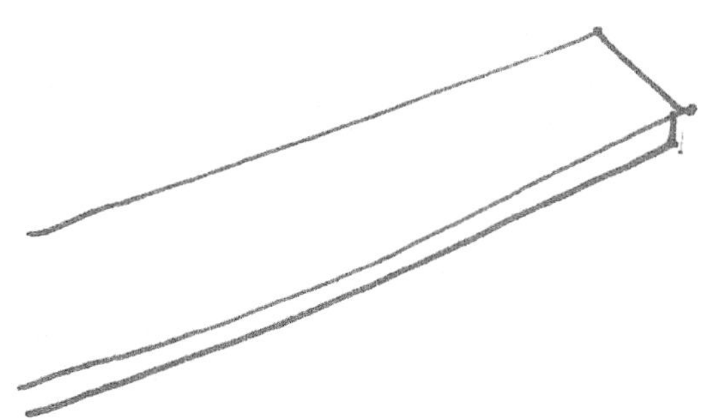

CREATIVE PROMPT

What's the most delicious dessert you can make with a cupcake, honey, and strawberries?

94

CREATIVE PROMPT

Where would you hide if you were teleported into the middle of a battle?

NAME

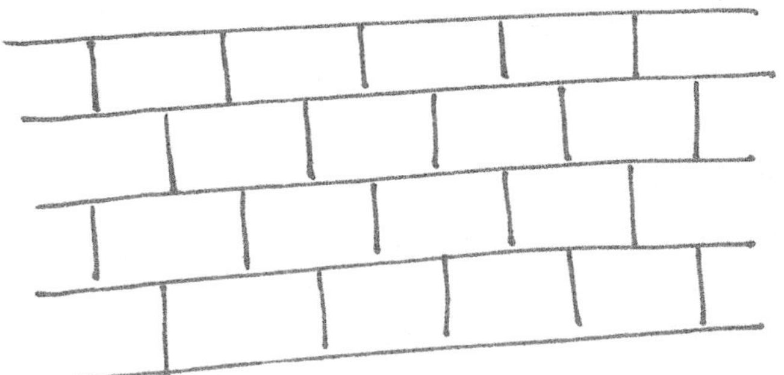

CREATIVE PROMPT

What would you bring to a BBQ at the North Pole?

NAME

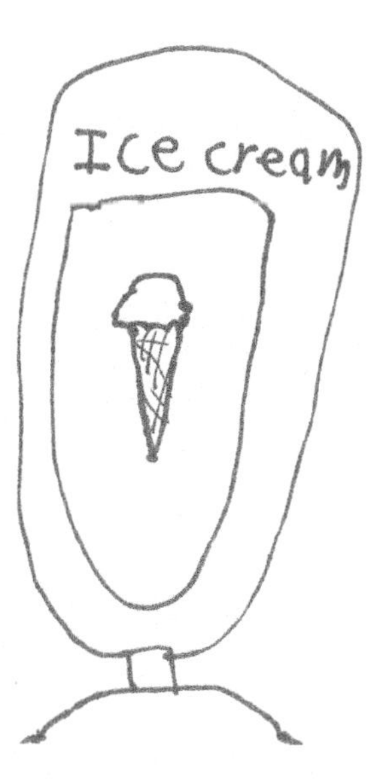

Ice cream

Describe how you would attempt your craziest water skiing stunt

IDEA
NAME

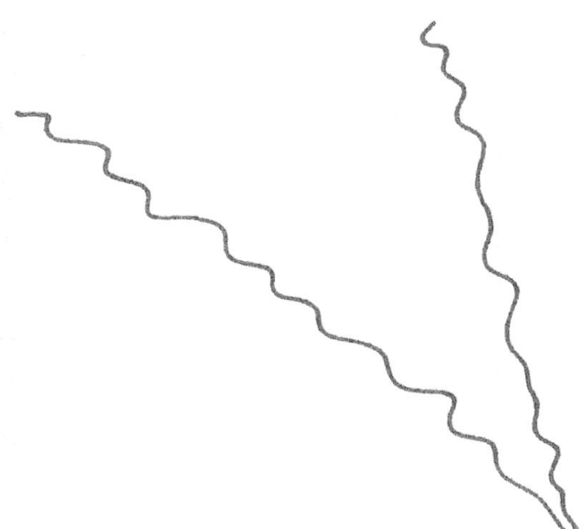

CREATIVE PROMPT

What would your car look like if there were no roads?

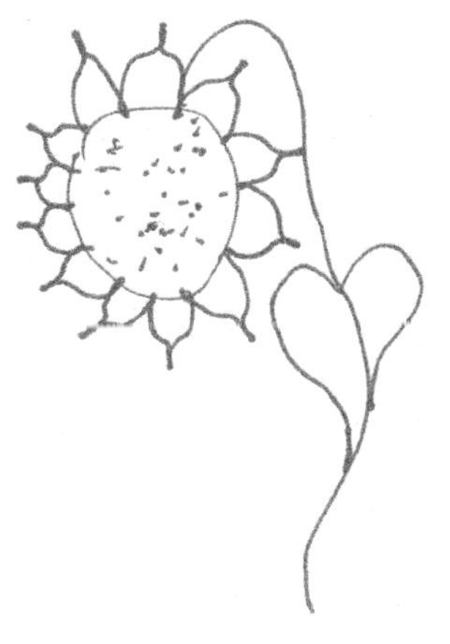

Spark

CREATIVE PROMPT

Create your own rollercoaster. What makes it magical?

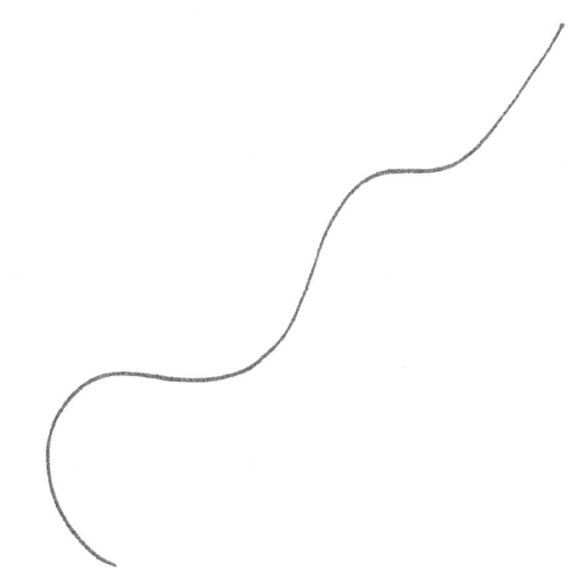

Spark

CREATIVE PROMPT

You have been hired to redesign the Princess room at the royal palace. She likes items from fairy tales

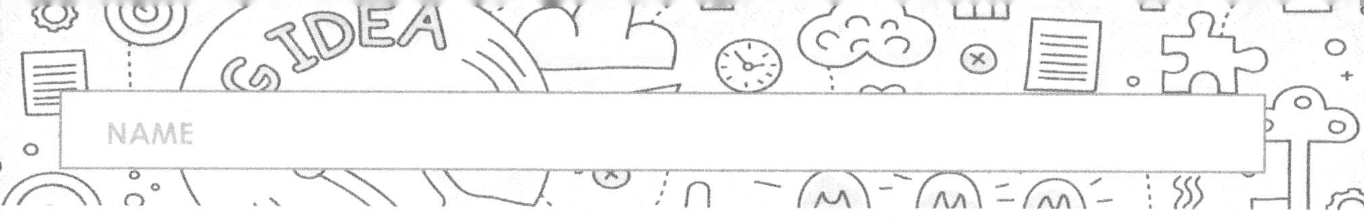
NAME

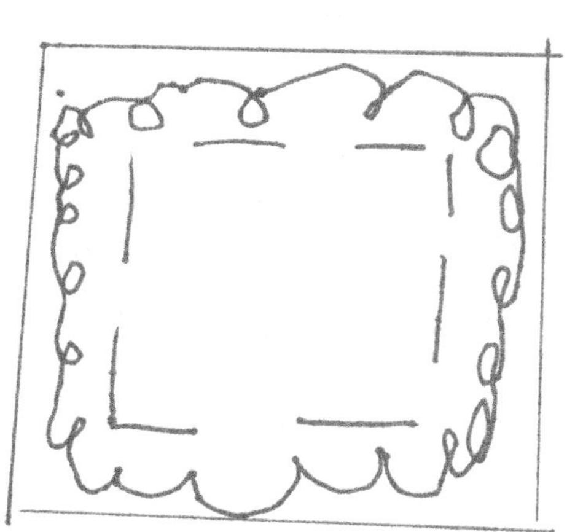

Your friend asked for the biggest-cake-ever for her birthday. Can you make one?

CREATIVE PROMPT

You just arrived at a gala at the White House. Who else is with you?

IDEA
NAME

NAME

CREATIVE PROMPT

What would cars look like if there were no roads?

IDEA
NAME

CREATIVE PROMPT

If you could choose, what would you include in the list of Seven Wonders of the world?

IDEA
NAME

CREATIVE PROMPT

What would an astronaut do with a dry erase marker in space?

IDEA
NAME

Where would you hide if you were teleported into the middle of a battle with Napoleon's army?

NAME

CREATIVE PROMPT

What's the farthest place you would like to visit?

IDEA
NAME

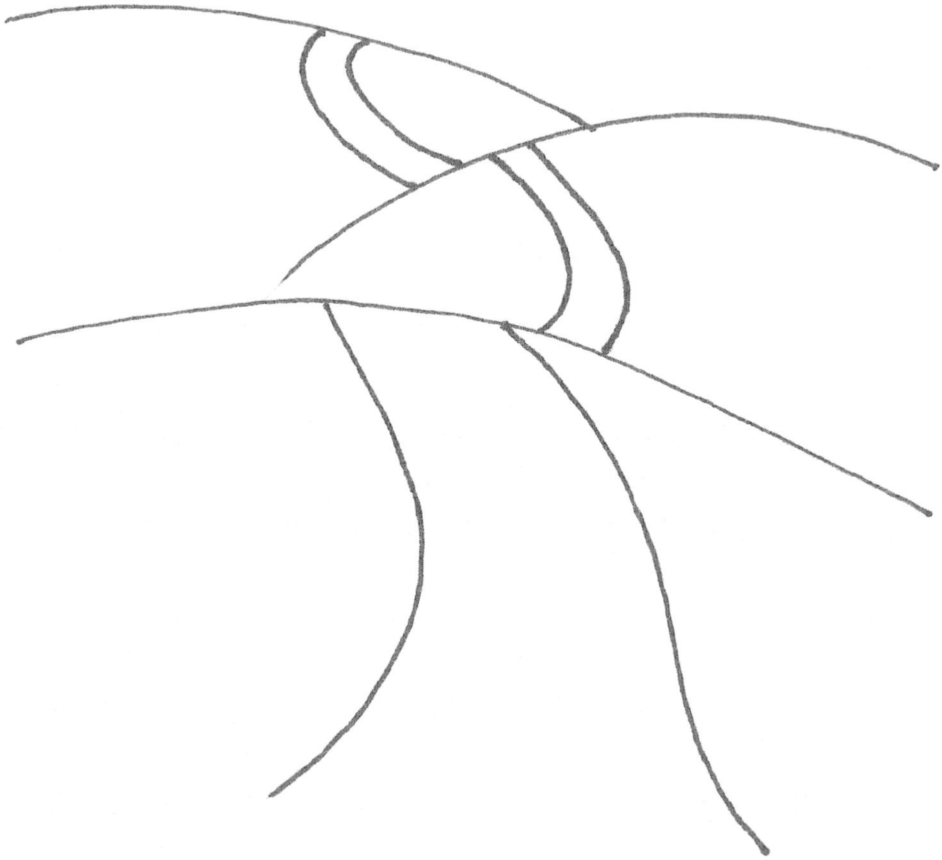

Can you create your own fairy tale?

IDEA
NAME

What is your favorite beach activity?

IDEA
NAME

 CREATIVE PROMPT

What one thing would you like to have if you were stranded on a desert island?

NAME

CREATIVE PROMPT

You have Superman, Shrek and three Minions for dinner. How do you prepare the table and what's on the menu?

NAME

lets eat

NAME

CREATIVE PROMPT

You were planning a stroll at the park, and instead this happened..!

NAME

Your neighborhood is building a local zoo. What animals would you like to include?

NAME

CREATIVE PROMPT

You just lost your cellphone at the water park. Where can it be?

NAME

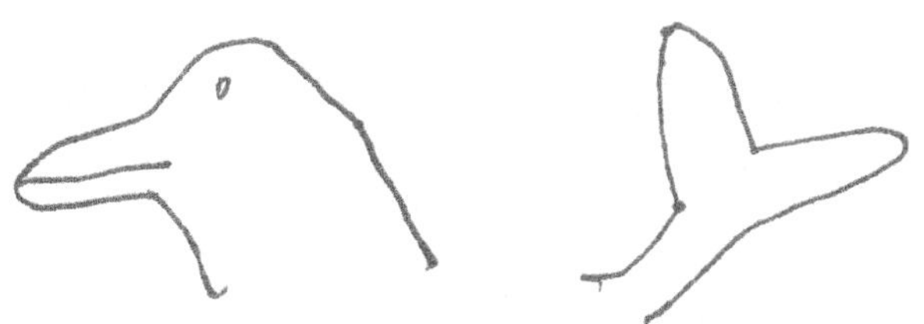

CREATIVE PROMPT

You just woke up and your last dream is still vivid in your memory. Draw it before it fades away!

IDEA
NAME

CREATIVE PROMPT

Aliens just arrived to Earth. They love tomatoes and seem friendly. What do they look like?

NAME

CREATIVE PROMPT

The national football team got stranded on the highway when their bus broke down. They are knocking at your door... how can you entertain them?

NAME

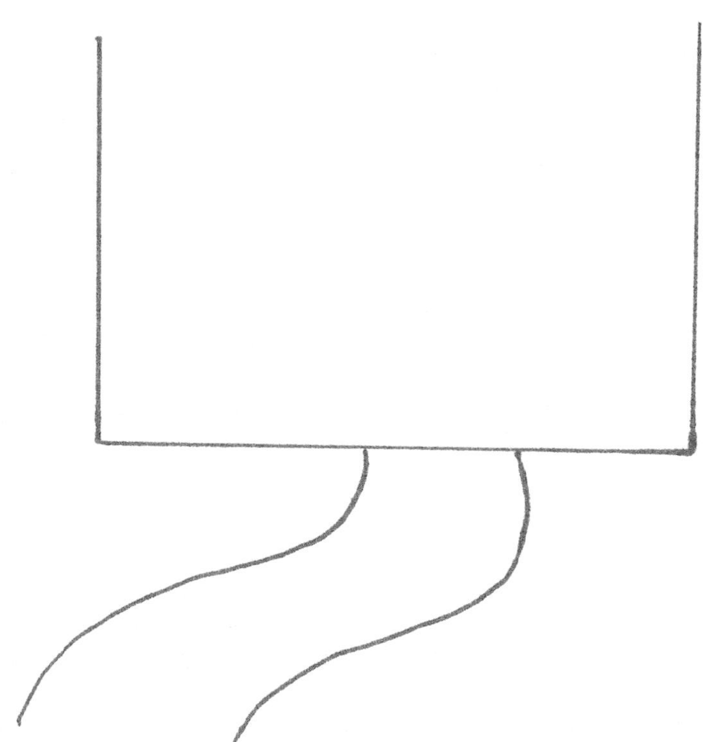

The invisible man is stealing your TV. How can you catch him?

IDEA
NAME

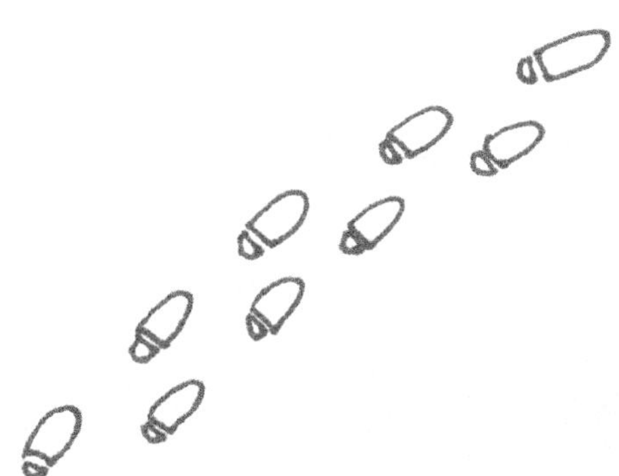

CREATIVE PROMPT

You are going to a costume party at the zoo. What outfit would you wear to avoid being recognized?

NAME

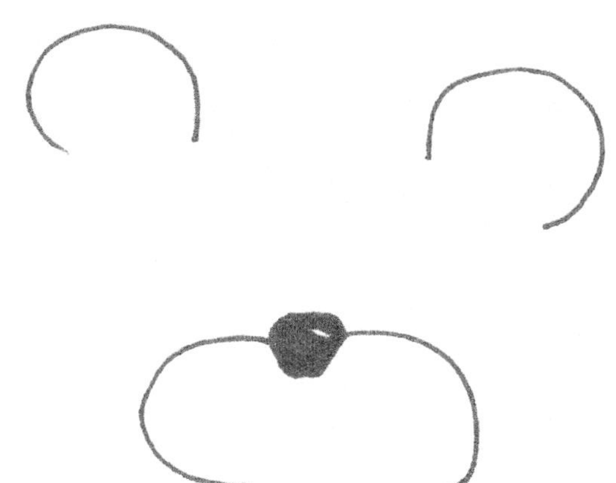

CREATIVE PROMPT

Where would you go with a flying carpet?

IDEA
NAME

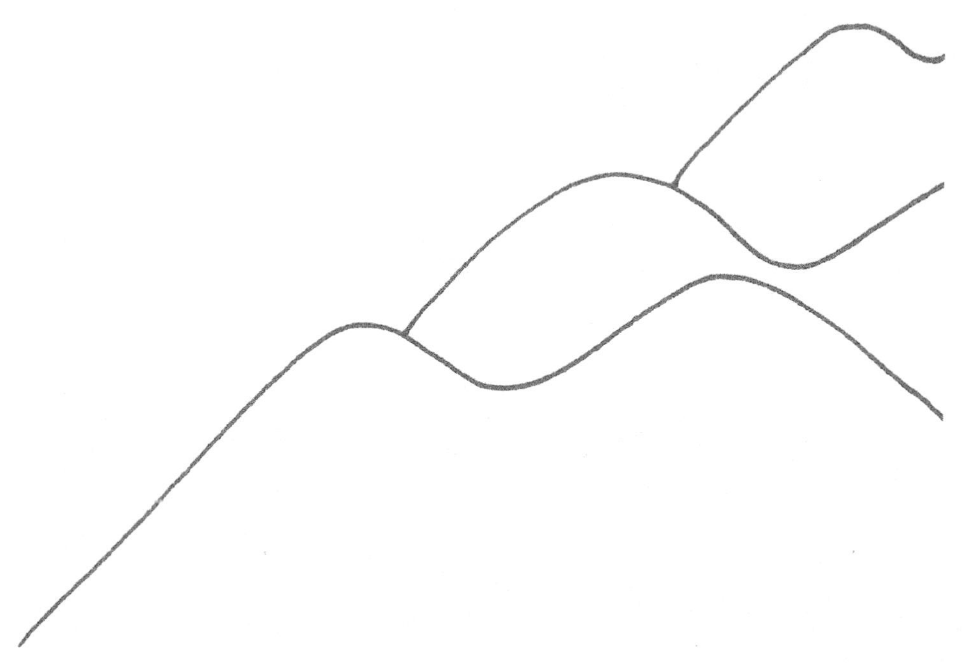

CREATIVE PROMPT

How can you make bombs that do something useful?

IDEA
NAME

NAME

CREATIVE PROMPT

Someone delivered an unexpected package at your door. When you open it, what do you find inside?

IDEA
NAME

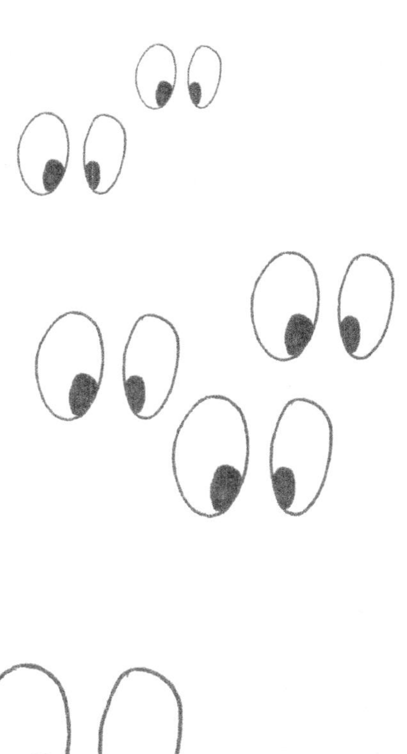

CREATIVE PROMPT

How can you turn a night in Alcatraz into something fun?

IDEA
NAME

CREATIVE PROMPT

How would you celebrate your fanciest birthday?

IDEA
NAME

Create a cartoon where the character just discovered a hidden treasure

NAME

CREATIVE PROMPT

During a tour around the world in a submarine you see a strange thing in the water. What do you see out the windows?

IDEA
NAME

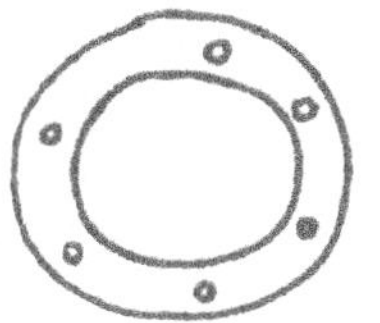 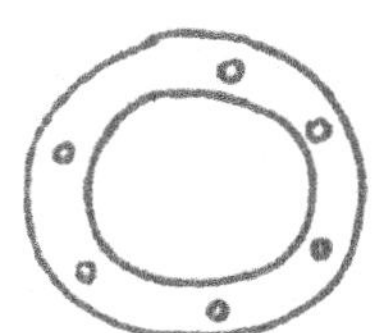 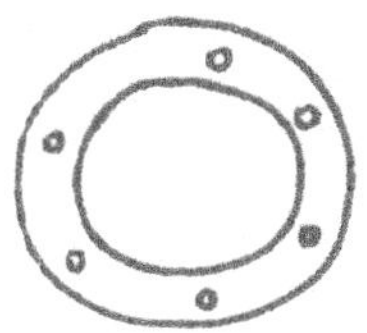 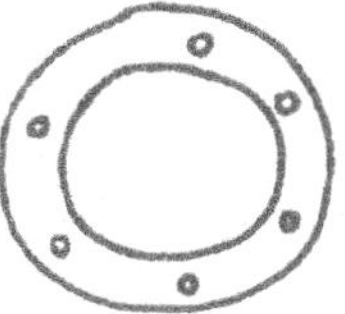

What is that bicycle-shaped object doing up there?

IDEA
NAME

How would you drive a toy car to work?

IDEA
NAME

CREATIVE PROMPT

What's one of the craziest things you have ever done?

163

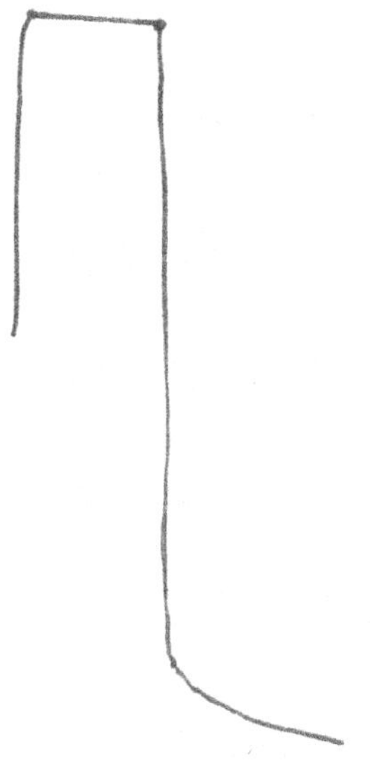

What's one of your favorite things to do when you are on an adventure?

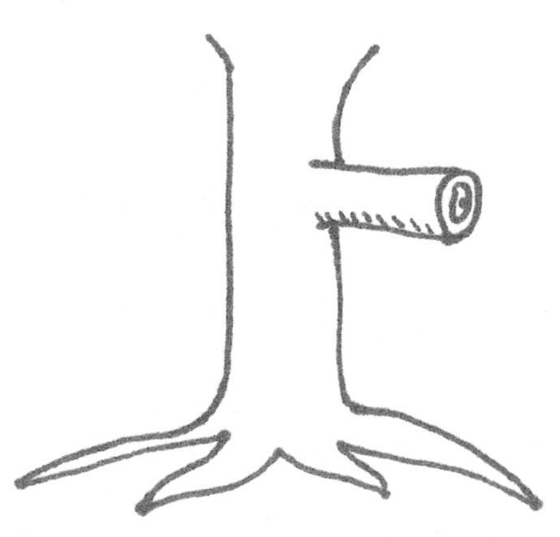

Spark

CREATIVE PROMPT

What would you do if you won $1,000,000?

IDEA
NAME

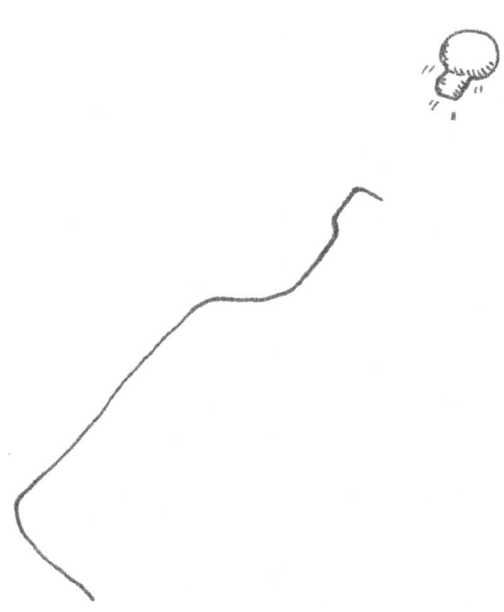

CREATIVE PROMPT

You open a box and find your favorite children's book inside. It starts talking to you...

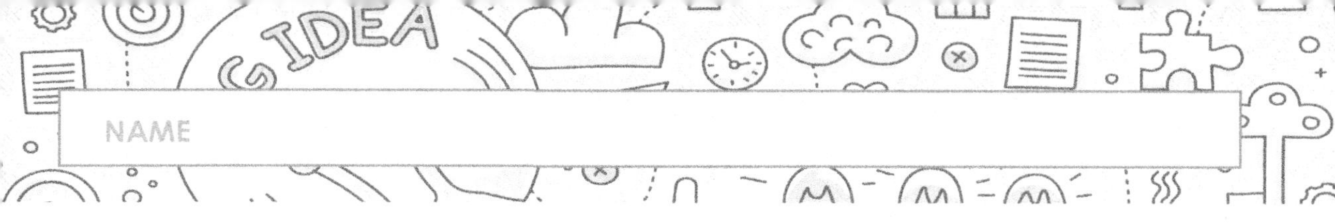
IDEA
NAME

CREATIVE PROMPT

What would you pack for a trip around the world?

171

You have been selected to design the next rollercoaster in your town. How can you make it memorable?

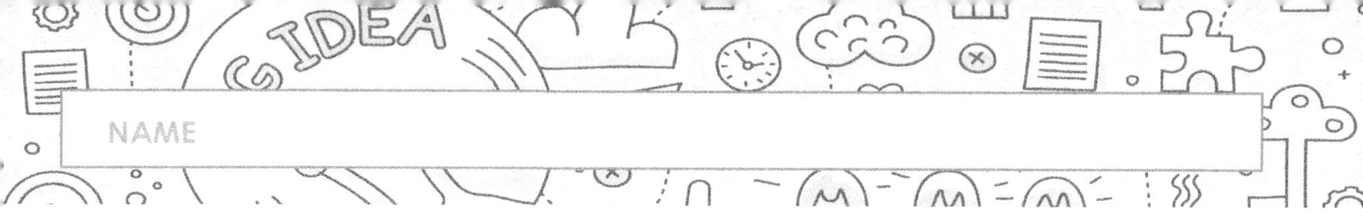
NAME

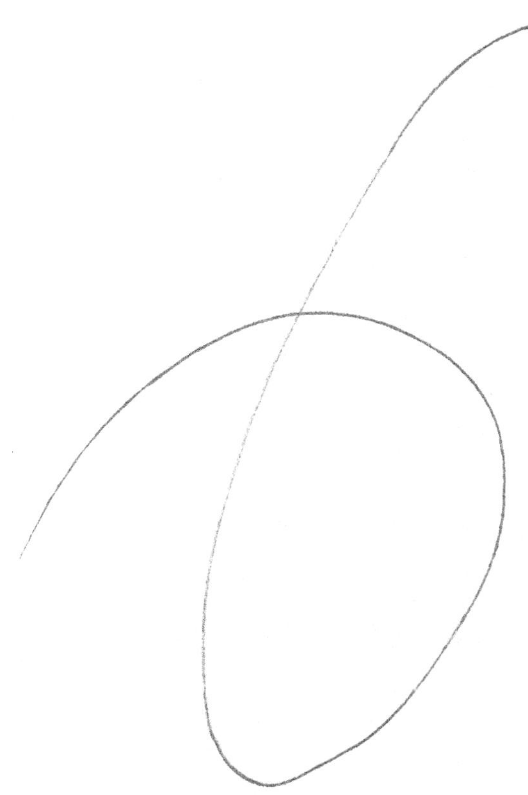

You just met two aliens at Mc Donald's. They look excited

Spark

CREATIVE PROMPT

What is your favorite thing to do when you have time to relax?

IDEA
NAME

Boom

CREATIVE PROMPT

Where would you like to fly to?

IDEA
NAME

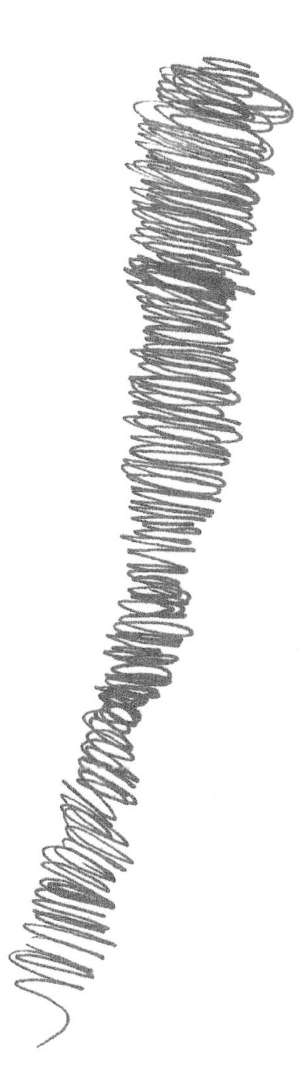

CREATIVE PROMPT

What would you say to a ghost who skips the line at the post office?

CREATIVE PROMPT

Make your favorite drink. How can you make it memorable?

NAME

We hope you enjoyed it!

We plant one tree for every copy sold

We are happy to work with ForestPlanet and their network of tree planting partners to implement our tree planting program. Please visit ForestPlanet to learn more about this amazing organization. ForestPlanet.org

ForestPlanet

Made in the USA
Coppell, TX
22 August 2022

81810533R10109